Sleepover Secrets

Beauty Blitz

Stephanie Turnbull

A+
Smart Apple Media

Published by Smart Apple Media, an imprint of Black Rabbit Books
P.O. Box 3263, Mankato, Minnesota, 56002
www.blackrabbitbooks.com

Printed in the United States of America, at Corporate Graphics
in North Mankato, Minnesota.

Designed and illustrated by Guy Callaby
Edited by Mary-Jane Wilkins

Cataloging-in-Publication Data is available from
the Library of Congress

ISBN 978-1-62588-376-6

Photo acknowledgements
t = top, b = bottom, c = center, l = left, r = right
page 1t Yobro10/Thinkstock, c Africa Studio; 2 Gayvoronskaya_
Yana; border 4 and subsequent pages Jan Mika, 4 Dejan Ristovski;
5t Africa Studio, tr Evgeny Karandaev, 5l Kuttelvaserova Stuchelova,
br and subsequent Perfect Planning boxes Garsya, b Emilia Stasiak;
6 oksix, 7 xymmus, 8 Piotr Marcinski; 9t Prapann, l homydesign,
b Aigars Reinholds; 11l Dejan Ristovski, r Roxana Bashyrova;
12 wavebreakmedia; 13 jcjgphotography; 14t Wallenrock, l schab,
bl ULKASTUDIO, br Evgeny Karandaev; 15 Africa Studio; 16 Robert
Red; 17 Eugenia Struk; 18tl Ambrophoto, tr manaemedia; 19t Jenn
Huls, b ConstantinosZ; 19 background Ulysses_ua, t Jovan Mandic,
c Baronb, b Mat Hayward; 22 nito; 23 GVictoria/all Shutterstock
Cover clockwise from bottom left i9370, Ivonne Wierink,
SOMMAI, Yobro10, ConstantinosZ, Evgeny Karandaev,
Darrin Henry/all Thinkstock

DAD0061
022015
9 8 7 6 5 4 3 2 1

Contents

Time for fun!

Sleepovers are a great way to have fun with friends, whether there are just two of you or a whole gang. Why not choose a health and beauty theme? You'll go to bed looking and feeling fantastic!

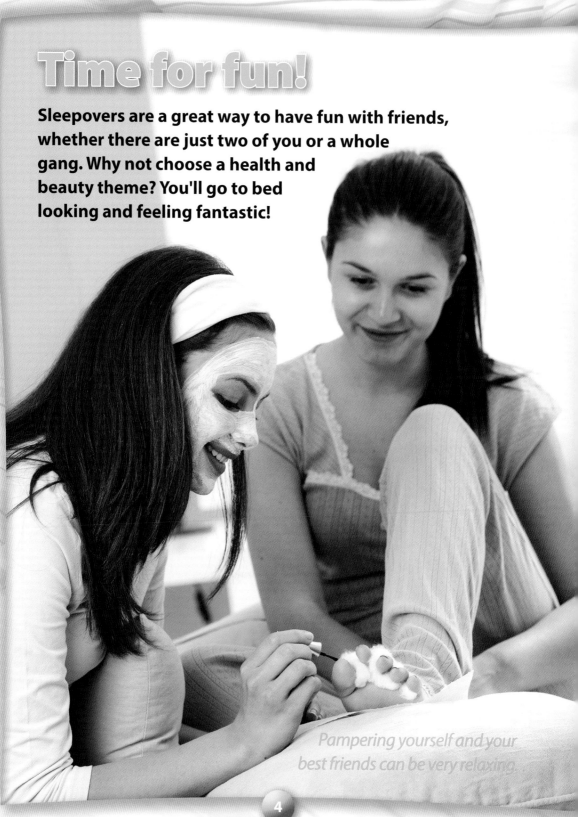

Pampering yourself and your best friends can be very relaxing.

Get organized

Decide which activity you'd like to try and ask friends their opinion, too. Collect the equipment you need and check with an adult whether you can use the kitchen or bathroom for messier crafts!

Make sure you have useful supplies such as brushes and towels.

Chill out

Beauty sleepovers are all about enjoying yourselves. Don't worry about who has the best clothes or most expensive haircut. And avoid makeup—it's messy, bad for your skin and **unhygienic** to share.

Remember good hygiene —wash your hands and face before and after your beauty blitz!

Perfect Planning

Send out invitations and list items you need friends to bring, such as nail varnish or soap.

Nice nails

Painting your nails is the perfect way to spend a beauty sleepover. You can help each other, then sit and chat while the varnish dries.

Clean and neat

Start by washing your hands and cleaning nails with cotton buds. File rough edges with an **emery board** and make all your nails the same shape—a squared-off oval.

File in one direction to create a smooth edge.

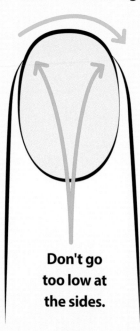

Don't go too low at the sides.

6

Nail art
Why use one color
when you could try two?

3. Carefully peel
off the tape to
reveal stripes!

1. Choose two shades that go
well together. Paint nails with
one and leave to dry.

4. Try diagonal stripes,
or sprinkle glitter on wet
polish. Dip the end of a
cocktail stick into varnish then
dot it on your nails. Experiment
and make every nail different!

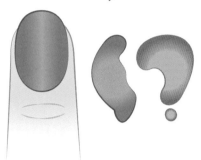

2. Cut thin strips of **masking
tape** and stick them on each nail,
then paint with the second color.
Leave to dry.

**Paint across
the nail, not
up and down.**

Perfect Planning

Buy clear nail varnish to
use as a base coat, or as
a top layer to add shine
to your nails.

Hair care

Why not turn your bedroom into a hair salon? Take turns to wash hair, comb it, and let it dry naturally. Put straight hair in plaits or curlers to give it waves, or try these ideas.

Pat hair dry. Rubbing it creates tangles and damages hair.

Tea treat

Conditioner gives hair strength and shine. Make your own by pouring hot water on two bags of **green tea**. Leave to cool, remove the bags and pour on to clean, wet hair. Leave for a few minutes then rinse.

Time to style

Give each other creative hairdos using hair clips, scarves, or headbands. Try this cute hair bow for long hair.

1. *Tie a ponytail on top of the head but don't pull the ends through—leave a loop like this.*

2. *Fan out the loop in two sections to make a bow shape.*

3. *Pull the end of the ponytail back and pin it under the bow with hair grips.*

Perfect Planning

Have magazines to read while you wait for hair to dry. Don't wash it so late that you have to go to bed with wet hair.

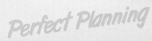

Super skin

Looking after your skin is important, so try a few skincare creams. Even better, make your own refreshing face masks—and have a giggle at how silly you look!

Be prepared!

This activity is messy, so make sure everyone ties back their hair and covers clothes with an apron or a towel around their shoulders. Use the kitchen or bathroom, where spills can be cleaned up easily.

Fruity faces

1. *Spoon a large dollop of thick* **Greek yogurt** *into a bowl, then add a chunk of ripe banana and a few strawberries. Mash well.*

2. Ask everyone to wash their face with warm water and soap or **cleanser**, then work in pairs to pat the mixture on to your faces.

Avoid eyes and mouth.

3. Let the mixture harden. Leave it on for 15 minutes, then wash off with warm water, and splash your face with cold water.

4. Use different ingredients to make more face masks, such as ripe avocado, watermelon, tomato, oatmeal, and honey. Throw away used mixtures; don't eat them!

Put cucumber slices over your eyes—they make your skin feel cool and relaxed.

Perfect Planning

Check that no one is **allergic** to ingredients —strawberries can give some people a skin rash.

Lovely lips

Lips can become dry and cracked, especially in cold weather. Follow these top tips to keep your lips soft and beautiful.

Think healthy

Eating healthily helps to keep skin—including lips—soft and smooth, so why not munch fruit or whip up a batch of smoothies? Drink plenty of water and smear on **petroleum jelly** or **medicated** lip balm to protect your lips.

Jazzy gel

Be creative and make your own flavored lip balm.

1. *Put a spoon of petroleum jelly into a microwavable bowl, melt in the microwave for about 40 seconds, then stir until liquid.*

2. *Mix in a spoonful of strawberry milkshake powder, then pour into a small pot or plastic lid. Leave to set.*

The bowl may be hot.

3. *Give everyone a cotton bud to apply the balm. Don't use fingers as they spread germs.*

Perfect Planning

Buy several milkshake flavors to make more lip balms, or try a few drops of food coloring or vanilla extract.

Feet treats

Don't forget your feet—they need pampering, too! Soaking your feet in a warm footbath is a wonderful way to relax tired muscles and soften hard skin... and your feet will smell gorgeous.

What you need

Find large plastic bowls or ask friends to bring their own. Arrange them so you can sit comfortably and chat while your feet soak. Pour in warm water from a pitcher. Be careful it's not too hot!

Nice and natural

Try adding a few soothing ingredients to your footbath. Milk and honey work well. Pour half a cup (120 ml) of runny honey and 4 oz (120g) of powdered milk into the water and stir until it **dissolves**.

Tea time

Tea, herbs, and fruit peel make gentle, sweet-smelling soaks, but put them in a bag.

1. *Cut a foot off a pair of tights to make a bag.*

2. *Snip the tops off three green teabags and pour into the bag. Add a tablespoon of freshly grated ginger and the grated rind of a lemon.*

You don't need the rest of the tights.

3. *Tie the top, put in your footbath and pour on warm water.*

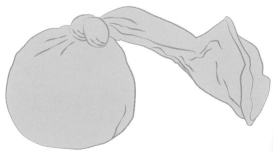

Perfect Planning

Hunt out other **herbal teas** so everyone can try a different soak.

Soap crafts

Perfumed soaps make your skin smell wonderful—and they're fun to collect and share, too. Why not test a few, or try these fun crafts?

Soap fish

Turn large soaps into funky fish to give as gifts or tuck in a drawer to make clothes smell sweet.

1. *Fold a large square of net in half.*

2. *Wrap it around an oval soap and fasten with a hair tie.*

3. *Decorate with googly eyes, ribbon, shiny stickers, and colored pins.*

Make sure the sharp pin points don't stick out of the soap.

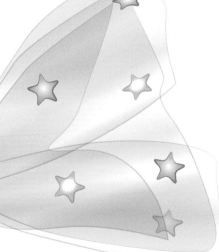

Make your own

Combine a few scented, colored soaps to create your own. You could even add drops of perfume.

1. *Grate part of each soap into a large bowl.*

2. *Add water, a few drops at a time, until the mixture is soft enough to squash into a ball, like dough.*

3. *Mold the soap into shapes or press it into cookie cutters.*

Perfect Planning

Find scraps of material and bits of ribbon or lace, then wrap soaps as pretty gifts.

Fitness fun

Give your body an all-over beauty boost with exercise! It's fun to get fit with friends, and you will feel stronger, healthier, and happier.

Don't slump on the sofa all evening —get up and around!

Get ready

Is there space in your bedroom to exercise to a fitness DVD, or could you skip or play tag outside? Warm up first to loosen muscles and get your heart pumping. Don't do anything that hurts or makes you too out of breath.

Try jogging on the spot, raising your legs higher with each step, then do gentle stretches.

Be helpful!

Why not work together to wash your mom's car, rake up leaves in the yard, or take the dog for a walk? It's all good exercise and you might earn a few treats from your grateful family!

Wear comfortable shoes and clothes for walking.

TV workouts

You can even exercise while watching TV. How about dancing during commercials, or doing special moves such as hops when an animal comes on the screen or star jumps whenever a certain character speaks?

Perfect Planning

If you go outside, lay out balls, hula hoops, Frisbees, skipping ropes, and so on, then take turns to play with them.

And relax...

To glow with health and beauty you need to relax. This doesn't mean vegging out in front of a computer or sprawling on the bed texting—it means feeling calm and composed.

Ditch the stress

Make sure everyone is sitting comfortably. Switch off music and other distractions, then close your eyes and imagine a relaxing place. You could be floating in space, basking on a beach, or swaying in a hammock in the garden.

Breathe slowly and relax every part of your body.

Perfect Planning

Try relaxing activities at the end of the evening to get you in the mood for sleep.

Amazing massage

A soothing hand massage is great for relaxation. Use a little hand lotion if you like.

1. *Take a friend's hand and make lots of gentle circular strokes with your thumbs, up to the wrist and down to the fingers.*

2. *Run your thumbs slowly but firmly down the hand and between the fingers. Do this a few times.*

3. *Make more circular thumb strokes down each finger, squeezing as you go.*

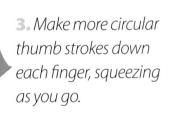

4. *Finally, make circular strokes all over the palm.*

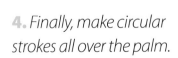

Glossary

allergic
Extra-sensitive to something, which causes your body to react badly, for example feeling itchy, sneezing, or getting a skin rash.

cleanser
A gentle lotion or cream for cleaning skin.

conditioner
A creamy liquid rubbed into wet, clean hair and rinsed off to help make it shiny and smooth.

dissolve
To become part of a liquid, without any bits or lumps left.

emery board
A strip of thin wood or card with a rough, grainy surface used to file down or shape nails.

Greek yogurt
An extra-thick type of yogurt that has been strained so it no longer has the watery, milky part (called whey).

green tea
A type of tea, originally from China, containing vitamins and minerals that are good for your body.

herbal tea
Any tea made from the fresh or dried leaves, flowers, seeds, and roots of different herbs, spices, or other plants.

masking tape
White sticky tape that is easy to cut into strips and peel off again.

emery boards

medicated

Something that has medicine in it. Medicated lip balm contains ingredients that help stop lips from cracking, plus a sunscreen to protect them from the sun's rays.

petroleum jelly

A clear or pale-yellow ointment that creates a waterproof coating when smeared on lips or skin.

unhygienic

Something that isn't clean and that may spread illness or disease.

petroleum jelly

Websites

www.helensstyle.com/nail-designs

Look at amazing nail varnish designs and watch video tutorials on how to do them.

www.longlocks.com/hair-care-recipes-cookbook.htm

Find lots of ideas for making your own natural shampoos and conditioners.

www.monkeysee.com/play/1494-fitness-for-kids-warm-up-routine

Watch short videos to help you warm up and exercise properly.

Index